SITTERS

SITTERS
Tony Roberts

2002

Published by Arc Publications
Nanholme Mill, Shaw Wood Road
Todmorden, Lancs OL14 6DA

Copyright © Tony Roberts 2002

Design by Tony Ward
Printed by Antony Rowe Ltd.,
Eastbourne, East Sussex

ISBN 1 900072 92 0

Acknowledgments are due to the editors of the following journals in whose pages some of these poems first appeared: *Envoi, Illuminations, Leviathan Quarterly, London Magazine, Modern Painters, Outposts, Poetry Durham, Poetry Nottingham, Poetry Review, Prop, South Coast Poetry Journal, The Spectator*.

'Poem for a daughter waiting by the telephone' was shortlisted for the Arvon International Poetry Competition 2000, and appeared in the winners' anthology.
'The Fan' won first prize in the Manchester Poets Open Competition 2000.

To Katy and Daniel,
and for Linda

The publishers acknowledge financial assistance from Yorkshire Arts Board

CONTENTS

These Few Lines about Your Eyes / 7
Rosa Meissner at the Hotel Rohne / 8
Painted Lady / 10
Love Poem in the Temporary Absence of Children / 12
Sitters / 13
Talk and Rain / 16
At Fredericksburg, with Children / 17
The Doll's-Eye Maker / 19
A Fiction of Father / 21
Peter Lorre bewitches My Mother
at the Manchester Hippodrome / 22
R.L.S. / 23
Grandparents / 24
Shady Characters / 26
Confederates / 28
Bonnard's Woman / 30
Mon cher ami / 32
Mamie Dickens in the Presence of Magic / 33
Of Nectar and Neglect / 34
The Fan / 35
The Language of Kept Flowers / 38
Moth / 40
Genius / 41
Son / 43
Poem to a Daughter waiting by the Telephone / 44
Postcard from Dublin / 45
Moondance / 46
The Lesson of the Master / 47

About the Author / 53

THESE FEW LINES ABOUT YOUR EYES
for Christine, nearing 40

If I tell you that your eyes
become more beautiful each year,
then you'll bat them, cross them,
tell me it's no recompense
for needing contact lenses,
or for all their lines.

If I tell you that your eyes
become more beautiful each year,
I'll see the light cavort in them;
you'll roll them and you'll widen them,
or else avert them winningly
and turn the conversation round to me.

If I tell you that your eyes
become more beautiful each year,
you'll focus them quite suddenly,
then narrow them suspiciously,
and tell me it's the place all right
but, lover, past the time.

So I'll just lie here silently,
innocent of devilry.
I'll look into those eyes of yours,
and improvise these lines of mine.
Till, sensing scrutiny you'll say,
'Now what's that in your beard – grey?'

ROSA MEISSNER AT THE HOTEL ROHNE
on an experiment by Edvard Munch in using mixed
exposure time to create 'spirit photography'

1

I posed for him in grubby rooms,
unsure *that* day because he meant
to capture with his camera
the spirit world where loved ones went.

He romanticised it like his Art
('My Intoxication', 'My Disease').
He was living by the bottle then,
neglectful of the niceties.

In Warnemünde, this, in 1907,
Olga thriving on sea air.
With her he played the gentleman –
Vergissmeinnicht – being debonair.

To me he claimed his money
would not reach to grander rooms.
Yet it stretched amongst the bottles,
came to rest on other bosoms.

He seemed impatient to begin,
then promptly left to 'buy cigars'.
Two hours. Three hours. Olga and I,
we talked the pattern off a vase.

2

Cheers.
Well, I am toying with the ghost of an idea.

I have been trying a little experiment
with the small Kodak.
I wish to so manipulate this box of tricks
as to make what is corporeal seem translucent.
A little movement, I find, works wonders.

Suppose the air is crammed with dead souls –
as Strindberg maintains –
would they look like this:

Behind Rosa
(standing in the flesh, hair pinned, head bowed)
I have the sister, Olga, dressed in white.
I instruct her to step in, then out of camera.
Welcome to the spirit world, I say.

Look at me: my hands are trembling,
learning all over again
how to paint with light.
I call it dying of exposure.

3

Try, but I cannot understand
the Desire that drives them, the Pain.
Why Art is a razor at their throats;
yet always the Desire again.

And as for me, without my clothes
I am a skinny thing indeed.
And yet great hands have pictured me,
Great Egos – men of little seed.

I held a pomander as we talked
that afternoon, and Olga laughed,
called me "altmodisch'. It stained my hand,
the hand not in the photograph.

He has it now – or it is lost –
the photograph; he went too far.
My sister, ghost in his camera;
such things are not for us, nicht wahr?

I saw his work last in Cologne,
at the Sonderbund; a lot was said.
Excuse me, but for me it hurt:
to know his mind, and Olga dead.

PAINTED LADY
Tuesday June 10, 1879

Dear George, to think I'd live without my tailor!
Yet I'm busy collecting specimens and labelling,
Mad as Von Humboldt blue-crabbing in Venezuela.

It's a great undertaking, a real headache
With the Wealth of Fluttering Life about –
A Lepidopterist's Paradise and no mistake.

Do you know, I was fighting off at dawn –
Literally having to fight off – a 'herd'
Of charaxes saturni – a 'herd!" One worn

Fellow splashed into the Dry Monopole;
Poor devil pepped the fizz up for a while –
Envious, really. Of course one couldn't be

At it all the time – one must be bellicose!
By the way, the war goes splendidly – e.g.
The ants have cleaned a fine skull for my curios.

Now then it's not the war it was at Sandhurst.
Zulu won't drown in Hennessey and hot air –
It's been earnest work here from the first.

You ought to hear the chump they made of me
Over that Kampula fight. There was I on all fours –
The air thick with death – clutching a Painted Lady.

I was blowing its wings out – shame to tell –
And would've sent my Totty for a net. When he found
I wasn't at death's door, the C.O. really gave me Hell!

Last week we found the body of the Prince of France –
My men took souvenirs of the bloodstained grass.
The poor beggar really didn't stand a chance.

"Though the death of a Prince brings emphasis
To our tenuous grasp on this mortal coil,
Won't an empty stool, or a farewell kiss?"

You'll sniff a cork in such Philosophy.
Meanwhile I'll metamorphose into Mars.
Imagine you're here to take a look at me:

Scuffed riding boots and red serge, carbine,
My helmet dyed to old field-brown with tea.
Don't we do our best in such gaudy times –

Imagoes all …… and you'll write to me?

LOVE POEM IN THE TEMPORARY ABSENCE OF CHILDREN

We make love in a drab room
splashed with the first sun of a rainy season.

In the bathroom, in the veined, discoloured bath,
in a pepper of damp sand,
are the shells we've collected with the children.

Later we listen to the traffic surf
between this grand, Edwardian hotel and the beach.

When you emerge from the bathroom, lost in towels,
you will evade my hands,

and when my lips touch the shell of your ear
you will hear those manic little feet,

remorseless, irresistible as rain.

SITTERS

"Will you be in England next summer? If so, I shall see you there, for I am to paint several portraits in the country and three ugly young women in Sheffield, dingy hole." (J.S.Sargent, 1884)

Dear Mnemosyne,
                It is escritoire hour,
And we are all busy scratching away.
Mr. Sargent arrived from the outside world
Four days ago. I had anticipated
Something reckless – a dove-grey morning suit,
Perhaps – but no; he's most agreeable,
Has a fine, dark beard, and gave me such a smile!   Mabel

"One prefers the Montagne Sainte-Geneviève
Set, to the toughs about the Opéra." S. –
How Mabel aches for either – Mere chit chat,
John Sargent! – I'm afraid that you won't do
With your glossy manners and your bric-a-brac –
You remind me of an empty sherry glass
(And Mabel reels from your effects) – Paint, man!   Clara

'Clara favours Art, and Mabel favours Artists,
    While I favour Life pure and simple.
Clara favours paint, and Mabel favours ribbon,
    But a young girl gets by on her dimple.'

Mama says I'm perfectly delectable
In my white muslin and blue sash. (She's lent
Me her turquoise necklace). I think so, too.   Florence

His French is exquisite – c'est magnifique! –
His German and Italian urbane.
He loves the theatre, devours romances,
And has taken to playing the piano
To lighten our sittings. Clara icy.

My portrait is shaping up…… but do I
Find him too discreet in his attentions?   Mabel

S. was somewhat tongue-tied in a 'that is
To say' sort of way, when we were alone –
It couldn't be he wastes his thoughts on me?
(One has to rage against unconsummated time.)
When this is over, Mama will sit for me
And then I shall sit for her – to that end
We are busy picking our guest's palette.   Clara

Was tremendously excited at first,
But am now bored flat – I hate to sit still
For hours on end, but enjoy being stared at.
I look like a chocolate box and the eye
Goes straight to me. (Not Nora's, which are crossed).
My two sisters sit like spiders spinning
Their silky satin webs in black and brown.   Florence

The portrait continues to dominate
Each day. Since it celebrates *my* 'coming
Of age', I am seated centrally, of course,
Wearing my favourite black dress.
Florence drapes me; Clara sits off to my left,
Straight backed and spiteful. My pulse is weakened,
I fancy – the after-effects of Love?   Mabel

'Art' and 'Heart'; there is barely a breath between –
John has such a firm, yet sensitive hand –
He paints in the Velázquez mode, and in
Sombre, winter fruitish hues – I pity him,
For Mabel sulks in sloe-black, and Florence
Sits fidgeting and sentimentalising
In her muslin cloud – *I* am very Reynolds.   Clara

M. and C. constantly bump and pass like
Dark clouds. Our guest is the electricity.
He looked seedy this morning (for lightning) –
Papa's mediocre sherry, Cook says.
I shan't fall in love with him, as I've been
In love too much this year (q.v. Feb., March, June)
And prefer gardeners to artists, anyway.   Florence

He boasts some singular observations!
In the garden he said our English sky
Moves too rapidly for him, and then he
Affected surprise at the size and shape
Of a cucumber! Poor Clara, to fall
For his oils. Yesterday he loved music;
Today he plays *Russians!* A slight headache.   Mabel

S. had the effrontery to deny
Leighton's greatness (and ignore my arabesques).
The portrait hands are strange – I see that now –
The light dramatic. We seem to sit before
A cave – He has failed to seize my ie self,
Which he obviously does not value
I keep to my room, where I read Vasari.   Clara

The deed is done, but not yet hung (or hanged?),
The Electricity packed up and gone.
But the strain of pretending how commonplace
His visit was! We are poorer by the sum
Of £400, it's rumoured below stairs.
Smashed hearts everywhere. Yet at least we have
The consolation of Immortality.   Florence

TALK AND RAIN
for Bruce, for Jim

"It's 2 a.m. out here." You're right.
I make the clock out, grab the beers,
cutting a sudden wedge of light
with the fridge door; my blindness clears.

I half expect to find his grass,
behind a stack of "Grateful Dead".
The slip of beer down beaded glass;
I navigate your chairs instead

and catch the fuzz of lowered chat
as I move amongst the books and things,
and then a note of weariness that's
coming from the old porch swing.

So what has changed since '72,
when two of us were students here,
and spent our mongrel time with you,
professor, chasing books with beer?

Tonight being with you is the high,
not weed, nor girls, nor raising cain.
Just crickets, tree frogs, Budweiser dry,
and hour on hour of summer rain.

I round the sofa, almost trip
on your ballerina daughter's shoe.
I bump the screen door with a hip;
it wheezes as I push on through,

hand out the beers, then take a pee;
you're trashing next week's Redskins' game.
That 'limey bastard' must be me.
It's good to know things stay the same.

AT FREDERICKSBURG, WITH CHILDREN

The guide mops up the questions and then poses
    for my daughter's camera against the length
of famed stone fence. His hat's brimful of what
    the textbooks tell of Burnside's men and Lee's.
Though he's heard everything, we know he hasn't
    heard the rebel yell. We in turn have coped
as best we can with summer's gore and glory,
    with maps and facts denied those slender boys.
A small disturbance as our son is gathered
    by his mother's hand, his little fingers
worming stones out of this treasured Rebel wall.
    His mind is on the heat, the motel pool.

The water's still this sun-stunned afternoon,
    until the children take the pool by storm.
I nurse a bourbon in a plastic cup,
    while they are sharks, explorers, aquabats.
They come and go, wet footprints fading in
    an instant from the flags. My wife discards
her sunglasses, stretches, stands, and slips unseen
    by them into the pool. I watch her from my
stack of books, from "Mary Chesnut's Civil War"
    to a thousand soldiers' letters home.
It seems that I am here *and* there. I dress
    and drive the two miles to the park again.

It's wasted time. The dead are gone beyond
    recall. I cannot raise their spirits up,
nor block the Brady wet-plate with its ragged,
    bloody line. Instead I turn to wander
through the cemetery, where the dead have had
    their anonymity carved in stone. I flush
a groundhog from a patch of shade and watch him
    as he waddles past the cairns of cannonballs.
I rifle through some worn and rusted relics
    in a nearby store. This is the old urge:
to procure the past. But today the dead
    have shrunk merely to war: knapsack buckles,

minie balls. At that my mind moves on beyond
    the children watching Bosnia on t.v.
to the body of my wife as she stands
    singing, brown and soapy, in the shower.
I nose the Buick back out of the park,
    the sunlight making rainbows on my screen.
I park the car outside our motel room
    and watch the water in the pool. It seems
to breathe, to flex like smooth, unbroken skin.
    My plastic cup lies rocking to and fro
in the shadow of the poolside parasol.
    I think to pick it up, then think again.

THE DOLL'S-EYE MAKER
In conversation with Henry Mayhew, 1850, author of
articles on the lives of the London poor

There is a saying, sir, and one you'll know,
That Beauty lives in a Beholder's eye.
Well, Beauty's in our eyes – I'll tell you now –
Though there are many pass them blindly by.
Dolls' eyes we chiefly make, sir, humans' too,
Like these I bring you in the cases here –
'Our present stock of optics,' as we say.
Here's sky and sea tints, if my meaning's clear,
And black and hazel in the fellow – see.
I have to smile, sir, at your rearing back.
"Uncanny" I would call the sight of all
These blinkin' eyes; they take a chap aback.
And can you pick the ladies' eyes out – sir?
They sparkle more; they're more – what? – breathtaking,
While a gentleman's is steely, if you will.
But it's a rare trade, sir, is eye making.
An eye must sit tight on the ball, you see,
Or it won't move for hanging in the head –
Some do, you know, the cheaper ones – the French –
No good will come of them – the eye looks dead.
The eyes I make will stay the course for years.
They look a treat. I have a lady wife
Has worn an eye of mine for these three years.
And can her husband tell? Not on your life!
It's tears, you know, that wears an eye out. Still,
A good eye sees you through bad times, I say
(A little motto I have fondness for).
You know who needs them most, sir, by the way?
You don't? All right then tell me when you saw
A servant with one eye? You ain't, I'll bet;
Who'd hire the wretch? I halves my price for them:
One guinea straight. And all in all I get
Three hundred optics into heads a year,
Besides six thousand dozen dolls' eyes, say
(For both the gutta-percha and the wax).
So things is looking up – forgive the play;
I drops 'em in my chat, sir, cheery like.

The truth is, though, that people in the street
Expect the very least of them as pass –
A mouth, two eyes, a nose, the hands and feet;
They're not particular. Too busy see
To notice much. Why tell me, sir, when last
You saw what you were looking at? Ahem.
Will that be all, sir? Don't your man write fast.

A FICTION OF FATHER

He'd been papering Occupied France
with 'The Courrier de l'Air': "a jaunt."
Tumbling illustrated booklets over
Rouen when flak exploded in their face,
the orange bursting in the white. Out went
the radio; the compass jammed, leaving
my navigator father dispossessed
of those routines that calmed him down. Snafu.

Dead reckoning coming home. He watched
the Channel, stiff as wavy, brylcreemed hair,
through shredded linen on the fuselage.
Engines clattered; night chattered; Father mouthed
wet smoke and vomit, methyl bromide fumes.

I recreate this from buff envelopes
of his war service: letters, clippings, stubs
and passes, photos, "gen." Here, for instance,
is the demob diary in which Father
plotted only train departures, gifts he'd sent,
and coded states of mind – "Stockings. Preston.
6 and H." Three years of war had taught him
disappointment is expectation's twin.

Tomorrow I will put him on his train,
illuminate the carriage, frame his mood.
But for tonight he flies his Wellington
on that fainting July night in '43:
freezing, feral, fumbling and flak-blind,
a father lost this month – by his lost son.

PETER LORRE BEWITCHES MY MOTHER AT THE MANCHESTER HIPPODROME
Monday 25th July, 1949

Here's my German grandma warning Mother
of the little, bug-eyed actor women
gave a wide berth in Berlin. His chalk "M"
hasn't faded after fifty films.

This is Mother sitting on the sixth row
of the Hippodrome, six months gone with me.
She's addicted to her movie stars
and waging her own war on rationing.

Here is Peter Lorre. Chillingly polite,
his mitteleuropäisch whisper
is just perfect for Poe's "Tell-Tale Heart".
'Now this is the point. You fancy me mad.'

Here is Mother on the cushion's edge,
stained with chocolate creams and thrilled to bits.
She knows that all the stars bathe in champagne
from when she stalked the stage door with Irene.

This is Father, bless his cotton socks.
He's come to meet my mother from his shift.
She's practising her faces on the bus.
He too is sure the baby is bewitched.

And finally we've four performing dogs;
they're snarling at the actor in the wings.
He names them 'Typecast,' 'Addict,' 'Bankrupt' and
'Divorced'. Mother wouldn't like to hear such things.

R.L.S.

He cannot write – it is choking hot –
and sits an hour to the flageolet.
Visitors. He must interrupt
his talk with Claxton, the missionary,
on their translations. Eventually
the conch is blown for dinner,
a surly hour made bearable
by claret neguses and pears.

He begins then balls a letter.
There has been no exercise today;
he might at least have weeded
with the boy. Later he lies awake
for hours, watching the spark
of lightning over the ocean.
His prayer is to escape from dreams
with something he can publish.

GRANDPARENTS

'You won't forget us when we're gone?'

I can't,
though you are of your time now:
that world of aspidistras,
peg rugs and pipe spills, the bread man calling.

My grandfather,
63612 Private Albert Kirby,
King's Own Yorkshire Light Infantry,
earned his 'blighty one' at The Somme,
then met grandmother, Doris,
at a Salvation Army jamboree.

A man of infinite patience.
A painter and decorator so true,
despite two numb fingers on one hand,
that he could walk the paper across a ceiling
and call it child's play. Like whist,
like catching flies in a quick fist,
like wiggling his ears,
an apocalyptic game of draughts –
or being evasive when I urged him back
to a handful of days in France.

Grandmother,
good-hearted, all industry,
would set her table perfectly
on crocheted white damask.
She had her 'lawky moses', and her 'over yonders',
her shades of green, and sunny Yorkshire puddings.

I won't forget you, your soap-scented love.

And yet, perversely,
you come back clearest in adversity.

Grandma,
when you spoke of your life's bitterness
at being put in service as a girl
and Granddad,
when under-aged, tongue-tied and overwhelmed,
you walked those muddy lanes in Hell.

The Great War hung in darkness
in your glaucous winter curtains.
It hangs as I once did

upon your every silence.

SHADY CHARACTERS

I

He has hired the German grand piano for a second time,
At the rate of ten shillings a month, including music.
They have renewed their subscription to the newsroom
And to the circulating book-shop for her French romances.
With angelic patience the heat is bearable in rooms
The sun is barred from, but its breath is everywhere.
Tiny invalid, she sits all day in a dressing gown.
He waits upon her, refusing to enjoy himself alone.
They live on love, eau de cologne, the lighter air
And celestial cheapness of the city of the Medici,
On figs, ice water, melons cooled in Casa Guidi's well,
Or else they dine for next to nothing on thin soups,
Three courses, tart from the *trattoria* three streets off.
In the evening their modest terrace swims in moonlight,
Falling from the walls of the church of San Felice.
They walk and talk of Dante, of the English in Italy,
'Shady characters in a sunny place', the saying goes.

II

These lofty rooms
on the piano nobile
are Victorian once again.

This April afternoon
we slip the tourists
in the hectic streets

to sit on crimson sofas
in the drawing room,
browsing through Brownings.

After the great galleries,
this unforced silence
is a work of art itself.

The green walls are flecked
with gilt-edged portraits
of poet friends and saints.

I pray for one fine photo
from the three you've taken
of me by the fireplace.

The boyish guide aside,
it seems as if we've just
arrived only to find

that they've stepped out
to take the air amongst
their potted trees.

Shady characters
all right, we eye up
everything before we go.

CONFEDERATES
'Burn everything; yes, everything. Black crepe and a dead heart.'

Steady my hand and then dress my hair please, Seraphina. Twenty drops of my Elixir can hardly spirit me away, but it fogs my train of thought this morning. Never mind, I shall persevere a little later with this. What I would not give for the strength to go below, to busy these loose hands of mine.

A moment, please. A few more drops before you go. I have lost that blessed numbness of the heart. Where is the pencil? I must return to my endeavours shortly. How is my hair? Let me see it in the glass, please. In the glass… Lord! You have done what you were able, I suppose. Now this afternoon I must be left alone. My regrets to Mrs. Summersby, lioness of the Ladies Association.

You know, before the war we led a life of such frivolity; I see that now. A life of dressing, visiting, tattling – while the men were out philandering. Now we have no life at all to lead and yet our talk is positively Homeric. Mrs. S., for instance, once a fat red hen, clucking over cakes and tea. Now the privations of the hospital have rendered her Niobe. And all her talk is of necessities – tamarinds and arrowroot and such.

When the Colonel calls on his "thankless task" tell Malvina to make the old roué a present of the pound cake and the bottle of peach brandy. Tell him I received John's last note. This is what he wrote, Seraphina, these words – I have them about me – here: *"Now that it is surely up with me, / My dearest, dearest dear. / I'll drink my laudanum / And await you in Eternity."*

No poet, John, but such a beautiful hand. You can see that much, though you do not know your letters. And if I presume a little on your confidence, it is this Elixir of mine. Are you pouting, Seraphina? Please do not pout. Please smooth the counterpane. I will take tea now. Thank you and close the door behind you as you go.

So, John, I must speak with you. This last week since your funeral, I have begun to conceive of my whole life as a tarnished necklace, the beads fashioned of routine. That figure came to me last night. Odd how vividly I remember some things. Each morning I address my mortal face in the glass and then stare joylessly out on a riot of camellias and live oak. Better my dreams in which you rise from the woods of Chancellorsville. I see you striding through the library, purposeful as the bust of Marcus Antonius, with a strength made whole again.

And now I have my little news for you. Firstly, it is all up with me, also. An asp at my bosom, of which I never spoke – a tumulous thriving there and everywhere. Like Cleopatra I'm betrayed, poisoned. And so I have determined I shall drink my small, companionable bottle of Elixir dry – blue dolphins on white spume – just as you did in your final agony. Our bodies are our last, victorious adversaries. We are merely their unwitting confederates. We will not need them when next we meet, when Eros triumphs over Thanatos.

I might have added Priapus, might I not? This second asp I mention now since my time is short – though why I should seek to excuse my bluntness, I do not know. Your bastard was born yesterday; its mother, Beulah, died of a haemorrhage; the baby is sickly; may God take it back where it belongs. There, it is said! Brave words from a barren wife.

And now that silent knock again that is dull, plain Seraphina's... Put the tea things there and leave me to my own devices. Thank you; you have been perfect. What must you people be thinking of in such confusing times as these? Never mind. I shall not need your company just now. Steady my hand and off you go. Back to my note – to Amy:

'Sister, lest we forgive too readily: burn the letters; burn the papers; burn everything.'

BONNARD'S WOMAN

A second glass? He cannot be above
an hour. And then he'll find us sitting here
just like old friends. Move closer, please. The young
alone can flatter from across a room.

In marriage you will learn that with the years
a woman grows unnoticed by her man.
At meals, or in my bath with tiger's feet,
Or for a rucked chemise I have his eye.
But then he sketches as you smoke, Monsieur.

Of course it might be that you cannot tell
that I'm the woman on his canvases.
On those I have eternal youth. True love?
Perhaps. Yet he's an artist like yourself –
a man – and knows at what age light becomes
the skin. It is his shining palette draws
you, anyway, and not his precious Marthe.

Besides, we two live here alone. Who else
might he have always at his hand? I think
in fact he likes to paint me as a boy,
a round faced boy – do not demur. He steals
my hips – no, please, sit here. He steals my hips,
my bosom. Look! I have a figure still.
Or else he paints me as I'm bending down.
But that is 'Art' and I know nothing, yes?

Well, he's the genius, young man, ask him.
I merely listen and then throw a vase
de temps en temps – Ubu! Now down you get.

He should be back within the hour. A tiff –
a little thing – because I would not go
to Cannes with him – for rags! I would not go,
because outdoors I do not feel quite well.

It isn't in my bath, you see – my bath
in which I convalesce – but in the street
that I feel naked and unclean. Well then,
I have my reasons and I say just this:

I am much talked about – not in Le Cannet,
perhaps not, but certainly in Vernon.
I do not mean amongst the cognoscenti,
either. You see we were not married when
we lived in Vernon. 'Married'; must I shout.

They called me 'Bonnard's Woman' there. Of course
they didn't mean it as a compliment.
You smile? I married him the day I heard.

But I, who am described as "reticent",
have made you feel uncomfortable. Please.
Oh look, my hand's a butterfly; it needs
a firmer hand to calm it down. Monsieur?

At any rate… Another glass? Ubu!
I fortify myself with this. We women
have a right to wine; it is our blood and
our bouquet. The grapes are trodden down, you see.
To be an artist is to be a woman,
after all. That little flame which takes on death?

And now because – a car! Pierre, I think.
Monsieur, we do not talk about the drink.

Mon cher ami,

I have been thinking of Tiresias
    and how the good Gods blinded him
for catching sight of Artemis bathing.
    All my life I have painted Marthe
at her toilette. (Imagine if you will,
    that I shall soon be wearily
applying salves against the spasm which
    creates clouds in the eye.) If I
should lose my sight, I shall have lost this grand,
    effulgent, sweeping, southern light.
We're old, my friend; we know more than we see.
    And yet please keep a weathered eye
alive – in the event of Gods!   *Bonnard*

MAMIE DICKENS IN THE PRESENCE OF MAGIC

Best she loves, the convalescent daughter,
Watching her father in his study, writing.
On his sofa, quieting her dress,
She holds her shrunken self as still as death.

His concentration is an entertainment
In itself. He'll scribble with the goose-quill
For a while, then suddenly attack
The mirror with some wild expression

That in a moment will be caught in ink.
And then there is the crowd he fathers!
They spring from his imagination,
The pompous, odd and pitiful, to bustle

In the atmosphere. She alone remains
Invisible, pale, alert, resistible,
Wishing she were fictional, waiting for
The moment when her plight catches his eye.

OF NECTAR
AND NEGLECT

In 18
46
Benjamin
Haydon
wrote

When I paint
I feel as if
Nectar
Was floating
In the
Interstices
Of the brain.

When he blew
his brains out –
debt ridden,
depressed by
public indifference –
it was found
to be blood.

THE FAN
'Woman seated on a balcony, New Orleans', 1872

    You've fallen for my genius,
You say? Thank God that somebody attends.
    Well, time is money, so I've heard;
Sit here before me, cousin, with your fan –
    Shoo pests and take the cat – *le chat* –
Oh leave the cat! You've made a pet of me,
    The lot of you; you've buttered me
With all your sticky love until I buzz
    About like the rest of you.
Now what about this face of yours, my dear?

    First, Mattie, hold the fan like so,
Down upon the knee. *Voilà!* Now tilt your chin.
    The sun is hot out here today;
It plays upon the senses like old wine.
    Give me a pretty look at least –
Shoo children! You'll upset my box of tricks.
    No darlings, put that down, and then
Your uncle will not need to floor you
    With an uppercut. Never were
There urchins good and bad and bold as these.

    Tilt! Look interested. No, no!
You look as if you'd swallowed a small horse.
    Imagine that behind me stands
Your first beau, and that you are now the you
    Of then. Don't crane the neck; *tilt the chin.*
The chin – le menton. Better. Now bend the arm
    And that is all there is to do:
To hold that pose until nightfall and then –
    What? Ah? It's just my little joke.
(Estelle? Out here, dear, on the balcony!)

    What, must you *now,* this very moment –
When we've just begun? Well then, hurry back.
    Yes I will sit here; yes I will.
I will hold a conversation with *Monsieur Chat.*
    Off you go… Now, have we met, Cat?

I am the famous, *farouche* cousin, Degas;
    I'm sure you've heard of me by now.
Play with this length of string whilst I complain
    Of this and that… The light, for one,
And every blessed interruption here.

    I have to paint a face a day
And my reward is sticky fingers in
    My hair and sloppy kisses on the cheek.
But that is family life, you'll purr. All right;
    Then what about the sun down here?
No wonder everything is white: it's bleached –
    Except the quadroons, half-castes and…
(My pastel will be taupe, though, when it's done.)
    Monsieur, the time has come for you
To talk. Pray ask me anything… Live here?

    Although the women are divine
And just as empty headed as one wants,
    I couldn't turn my hand to work.
And painting relatives is not the thing;
    One's poor by such a family *debt.*
Besides, the light's impossi   . To catch
    A people's charm you need to spend
The time with them, to watch the way they live.
    Or what you've got are clever daubs,
Each short of composition: photographs.

    And anyway how could I paint
America, this land that's without end?
    Too much is new; while Art depends
On what it learns from repetition's eye.
    Yes, off you go; that pretty thing
Won't wait. Besides I hear my cousin's step.
    Your cat and I were swapping thoughts –
A clever fellow, I might add, who's leapt
    Over the railings to pursue
A tête-à-tête with a small butterfly.

    I empathise with that old cat.
Sit down and we'll resume. Remember, though:
    '*Patience passe science*'. Tilt the chin.

Tilt. Remember the beau. Where is the fan?
    I bought a fan in Paris once,
And gave it to a big-eyed girl who worked
    In a boulangerie. Each day
I passed I saw her sitting there, the fan
    A-flutter in her hand. Was this
Display got up for me, or for the flies?

    I am, you know, a catch, and that
Is quite enough to make them pester me,
    Despite my looks. Besides, you shine
And yet your sort of beauty only is
    To goodness what my talent is:
A fan to flutter, an apology
    For what is lumpy in the soul.
Ah, here comes *Monsieur Chat.* Please notice that
    His little mouth is powdered with
The dust that gilds the wings of butterflies.

THE LANGUAGE OF KEPT FLOWERS
In 1851 Elizabeth Siddal posed as Millais' drowning Ophelia.

12 NOON

She is floating to her death without demur,
Fantastically attired and garlanded,
In a tepid bath on Gower Street. For this
The artist had spent a summer on the Ewell
("Having gone to Nature in all singleness
Of heart') to paint that willow 'grown aslant
A brook'. With such fidelity to detail
Won't the critics quack! Now his Ophelia
Is the shop assistant Gabriel had picked.
Despite ballooning draperies and sodden
Trails of copper hair, he's caught her to his
Satisfaction in that bright, consumptive look.
They'll lunch on cake and sherry after this.

1 P.M.

Kind words are crumbs of comfort. My buoyancy
Like hers was momentary. Men know success
And disappointment even-handedly –
As one might say of this you're working on
Just now: "Such luminosity!" And yet
Another, walking in the room, might urge:
"Ones eyes are hurt for want of colour tone."
Well, women live their lives without remark –
Not all, but most. The privileged sit still
And wait for boredom to disable them.
Before I sat for genius I stood
A million years in a milliner's shop.
Now what is *there* to build a soul upon?

2 P.M.

Gabriel once said I was 'the image
Of his soul.' Can you imagine? The image
Of his soul! Only later did I wonder
What that left of *me* for *me* to cherish:
(I stir the water with my agitation.
Forgive me; I am often not like this.)
Canvas; vellum; a drawer of drawings
Colourless as soul on pure white ground;
'Ethereality', 'enigma' .
You laugh, my friend, but do you know I've such
A tenuous grasp on things that are, I think
They needn't be. I am Ophelia: idle, mad,
Drowning in the language of picked flowers.

MOTH
for George Good

A moth distracts me from my reading.
Persistently it dabs itself
against the window.

Chekhov lies dying
in a hotel room in Badenweiler.

He has all but put aside sensation;
it is the work attends.

Boots crushing gravel.
Olga's perfume clouding at his brow.

Despairing of camphor
his physician prescribes a last mild stimulant:
champagne.

There lies Chekhov,
all his vivacity in one last glass of wine

and the moth at my window,
his large heart,
dabbing against the darkness.

GENIUS

Shostakovich tells how Stalin
Sat in his dacha listening
To Yudina playing Mozart,
Then phoned the Radio Committee
For a copy of the record.

It had been a live performance
But they dare not own to that.
Instead they called out pianist
And orchestra. It took all night
With three conductors to record

The single copy. I imagine
These as grey men faint with fear.
Returning to their wives, they spurn
The samovar, and take their vodka
To a corner of the room.

The third conductor mutters how
In Mozart's time pianos
Offered no dynamic challenge
To an orchestra. His sense of
Irony is stiffened by the drink.

The second managed in his trembling
To confuse half the musicians
And clearly had to be replaced.
His thoughts are, more predictably,
On life and income, wife and home.

But what then of the first conductor,
Dismissed for being too scared to think?
Does he sit and listen to the pipes,
Search for faces in the wallpaper?
Or is his mind on how, returning

Late from the conservatoire,
He'd passed a couple '*doing it*'
Against a tree? 'What beasts!' he'd thought,
'To live amongst the appetites'.
And now, 'What simple genius!'

SON

We pick up his subdued friends
on their way to the cricket dinner.
Each stop I'm staggered again
by a new fusion of toiletries.

The scent will not leave with them.
When I park the car I still inhale
a musk louder than the rain.
"I am fourteen," it fumes. "Smell me."

POEM TO A DAUGHTER WAITING BY THE TELEPHONE

They say that Howard Hughes
kept some young flyer
at a lonely air-strip
in the scrub of the Painted Desert
waiting stand-by on a whim

and that the boy stood there smartly
the desert blowing in his face
tall and lean by the fuselage
his ears honed with listening
for the call that never came

while his lonely pretty wife
slowly fattened in her boredom
and the children grew up surly
in a big draughty house
with no father's back to ride on

until one fateful morning
when Hughes wrinkled to nothing
and the last cheque arrived
fluttering like a falling leaf
to the long abandoned doorstep

and the poor bearded flyer
dropped the rusted telephone
zipped up the scoured jacket
spat bleakly at his prospects
and stalled there in the sand.

POSTCARD FROM DUBLIN

'Our view is of O'Connell Bridge
and of the Liffey (no white horse).
Re-joyce-ing in the Guinness, kids.
We miss you terribly, of course.'

Lame wit, I wonder in our luxury
why ever we thought of having them,
those lovely, wilful children.

Late afternoon and we lie drifting
in our theme hotel, drunk with plans,
indolent with lovemaking.

The book I dropped lies belly up
beside the bed. We've borrowed back
those bodies gone for children's games.

At five fifteen, across the alley,
the dance studio kicks into life,
its music hamstrung by the monotone.

When the brindled curtain breezes in,
we're moved at last to warm ourselves
with counting our contentments:

a quickened marriage, a warm quilt,
that tireless comfort – man and wife –
of endless talk about the children.

MOONDANCE
after paintings by Winslow Homer

They are perched on bluffs at fashionable Long Branch,
    behind lorgnettes, beneath parasols.
It is neither breeze nor bustles tilts these beauties
    in their flounced skirts; they are not dolls.
Their self-appointed task is social vigilance.
    Or else they promenade in creams
against a blue-black sky. Behind their fans they speak
    of Lake Geneva, dwell on dreams.
Do not be fooled by pretty, muslin furbelows;
    these are robust girls who swim and scheme.

A summer night at Prout's Neck with the artist
    and his family. A moon-faced pair
of blonde young women waltz together on the porch
    (an afterthought, the dancing there).
The party, sitting on the rocks, looks off in
    silhouette to watch the light play far
across the ocean. To watch Wood Island's lighthouse lit
    like the last post-prandial cigar.
Unconscious of attention, gilded in porch light,
    these girls, untouchable as stars.

In season he will take the smoker to the North Woods,
    unpack his sketch block and begin to delve
into the little matrimonies of the hunt.
    He'll dishabituate himself
to Amazons, for it is in the woods one knows
    instinctively how one may helve
one's manliness. Here rules are clear; there's blood to show.

THE LESSON OF THE MASTER
"I gave Sargent this A.M. my first sitting for the portrait – *the* portrait."
(Henry James to his nephew, May 13th, 1913)

And now the sitting's almost fnished, may I talk?
    I dreamt last night you made me sit through lunch
until we faintingly achieved what Browning called
    "the grey remainder" of the day in his
'Andrea del Sarto' – a faultless painter
    like yourself, though ruined by a grasping wife.
It's really very good of you to waive your fee
    to get this 'Seventieth' portrait done.
Did Browning never sit for you? A man of *the*
    profoundest paradox; I readily
imagined there were two of him: the great artist
    and then the social bore; I wrote of it.

Of course we each of us are two and twenty two
    at least – twenty three including this… this… *me*.
I have to say it's been the finest morning:
    your wit, your music, your lovely, light-filled room;
my 'dolce far niente' and the river commerce;
    your charming, youthful garden, too… I take issue
only with your generosity, old friend.
    Here, let me take one last immodest look
at what you have accomplished this first sitting.
    Frankly I'm embarrassed to pronounce it fine.
You'd placed me in the first, auspicious hour, whereas
    I can barely place myself by lunch these days.

It's jolly hard for me to credit that you haven't
    practised portraiture for three, whole years.
Being at my most… expansive – in both senses
    of the word –I might be Johnson to your
Reynolds. In fact, I was thinking as I sat here,
    making as little of myself as – what? –
that though the artist in you shies away from such,
    there are commercial considerations
congruent to aesthetic, such as the desire
    of sitters to reduce themselves to charm.

In fiction, too, the same holds true. Yet there, at least
   one's 'clients' do not always want control.

I have maintained always – and do forgive me if
   I have maintained to you over the years –
the author and the artist are as one in that
   their mission is fidelity to truth.
We seek a likeness fresh from peering in a soul,
   whilst hinting at ambivalences there.
Reality is your domain, whilst History
   is mine… The tea is excellent, thank you…
And we have known each other thirty years? Let's take
   one turn about your garden as I leave.
We met at the Boits, when you had just painted that
   fine portrait of the girls – a favourite since.

Was it Henrietta Reubell introduced us?
   Etta, one's angel of introductions –
her bright red hair forever swathed in cigarette smoke.
   She knew everyone – including Oscar Wilde.
The world had barely lost my master, Turgenyev.
   And then you took me to your studio
on Boulevard… Berthier? I came to see
   your portrait of the Gautreau woman.
I remember best her quite amazing profile
   and a pallor, which I think she had achieved
by deadening the skin with arsenic. The organ
   of the ear was an exquisite, rose-pink shell.

Will others make as free, when they are talking of
   the *canvas* James, as we have done with her?
I should disrelish that. The Gautreau woman
   lived for such attention. Reputation
and perfume, she wore both recklessly. In your wild
   portrait this was palpable; hence the scandal.
The theatre was sufficient notoriety
   for me; so you may paint *me* with less noise;
Boswell if not Johnson. Enfin. Where did I leave us?
   … smoking cigarettes into the night
and talking… you'd been reading my books, or Flaubert's,
   or someone else who had a bone to gnaw.

These days I lack the stamina for great events,
    for Time has gone, indeed, and gone to prove
the artist fixes only shadows of a truth.
    I am ill; I cannot bark or caper;
yet my recuperative powers are the toast
    of London – which occasions 'visitations'.
Satisfactory as this is, as far as the
    aesthetic digestion is concerned,
they undermine my corporeal health, and leave me
    sans le souffle… and on the madness goes.
Dear Edith Wharton writes to me prodigiously…
    well, you would call that oxygen, perhaps.

And now let us turn to the interminable.
    Acquaintances are never tired of pointing
out that I, who am the author of a hundred
    women, have never yet quite married one.
The 'oversight' belongs to you as well, of course.
    In my defence I like to claim that marriage
is a fiction far too grand to be believed.
    I say I'm spoken for by Art herself,
by the blessed, sacred loneliness of Art,
    for you and I know marriage and the change
it brings: like age it wears away the layers of self.
    Protect the work; it animates the life.

I've a quickened fondness, though, for women.
    I thrive upon the atmosphere that's theirs.
Of course you have to skirmish with them to establish
    territory. Name one? Miss Woolson, then –
Fennimore – who fell from a Venetian window…
    It's now too chilly to walk out… Or it's
the Hand of Death upon my throat… You smile at that?
    Death's fearful blankness – no nuance left?
At any rate I've left aside the 'Passion', now;
    I've met my missed possibilities
and we are friends. A desiccated antiquity
    is what I've left. Basta! What have you found?

Ah, yes. A little notebook I now keep to prompt
   my memory – the Boits are here. Tonight?
A dinner – see – then Mozart. It won't appeal to you
   who favour the exotic... De-bus-sy.
You haven't touched a face in three years, is it?
   Then you may legitimately have feared
it wouldn't do to start by picturing mine.
   I have to say, however, that you've turned
up trumps and shown me how the painter fixes us
   while introductory pleasantries are served.
The true self potters in the trivial.
   Browning – somewhere – wrote about the soul

peeping over the glasses' rim at times of
   satiety. One last thing: to see
how others portray us is to take one fraught
   perspective on the central dare of Life:
the deciphering of self. But which self: Johnson?
   Boswell? You sit me grandly; I can't carp.
Besides, the artist and the sitter, which is which?
   I must go; *I must.* Someone quipped, you know –
hearing that I was sitting for you for this *grand,*
   celebratory portrait – I wrote it here-
'To sit for Sargent is to take one's face into
   one's hands.' I take my leave; the sitter stands.

TONY ROBERTS was born in Doncaster in 1949. He was educated at Didsbury College and then, on a Drapers' Scholarship, at the College of William and Mary in Virginia. A teacher of English, he lives in Manchester with his wife and two children. His work first appeared in the introductions volume *Peterloo Preview 1* (1988). A solo collection, *Flowers of the Hudson Bay*, was published in 1991. His poems have appeared extensively in magazines.